COMPILED BY
CHARLIE HOOKER AND JEFF ROBERSON

The Nautilus Publishing Company
426 S. Lamar Blvd., Suite 16
Oxford, MS 38655
Tel: 662-816-4949
Email: info@NautilusPublishing.com
Web: NautilusPublishing.com

ISBN # 978-1-949455-13-7

Publisher: Neil White
Editors: Jeff Roberson, Charlie Hooker

CONTENTS

THE EARLY YEARS

1. Who was the first football coach at Ole Miss?
A. Frederick Barnard
B. Alexander Bondurant
C. Robert Fulton

2. In what year did the university first field a team?
A. 1892
B. 1893
C. 1894

3. Bondurant first proposed an intercollegiate football team at the university in what year?
A. 1890
B. 1870
C. 1889

4. For the first football practice, with 30 students, Bondurant called for a 4-mile run. How many players completed the 4-mile trek?
A. One
B. None
C. Two

5. Bondurant convinced another man (one who had played football at Hampden-Sydney College) to travel to Oxford to help coach the team. What was his name?
A. John Heisman of Auburn
B. J.W.S. Rhea of Memphis University School
C. Pop Warner of Georgia

---

1. B
2. B
3. A
4. B
5. B

6. In 1893, Bondurant brought football tactics from what team?
A. Yale
B. Harvard
C. Rutgers

7. The Ole Miss colors were decided by Alexander Bondurant in 1893 alongside the creation of the football team. The notorious colors of Ole Miss are from two different schools. What schools inspired the classic red and blue?
A. Harvard and Yale
B. Michigan and Rutgers
C. California and Maryland

8. Ole Miss beat Southwest Baptist University in its first game. What was the score?
A. 56-0
B. 4-0
C. 2-0

9. The 1893 team lost only one game. To what team did they lose?
A. Alabama
B. New Orleans Athletic Club
C. Tulane

10. Scoring in college football changed regularly between 1893 and 1912. During the university's first four seasons, how many points were awarded for both a touchdown and a field goal?
A. 4 points for a touchdown; 5 points for a field goal
B. 5 points for a touchdown; 2 points for a field goal
C. 3 points for a touchdown; 7 points for a field goal

---

6. B
7. A
8. A
9. B — The NOAC was made up of "former college men." The students at Oxford lauded the fact that the inaugural team was undefeated against other college teams.
10. A

11. In 1894, Mississippi played Alabama in Jackson in front of 1000+ spectators. It was the first football game played in the state of Mississippi. What were the gate receipts for that game?
A. $2,000
B. $190
C. $0

12. What was the cumulative record for the university team during its first two seasons?
A. 10-2
B. 6-6
C. 3-9

13. In 1895, Mississippi joined the newly formed Southern Intercollegiate Athletic Association. What was the mission of the league?
A. To ensure the safety of players
B. The development and purification of college athletics throughout the South
C. To prepare young men for God, country, family

14. Enthusiasm for the football team waned in 1895 and 1896. What was the school win/loss record for those two years?
A. 3 wins; 3 losses
B. 6 wins; 0 losses
C. 0 wins; 6 losses

15. The 1897 football season was canceled. Why?
A. A yellow fever outbreak
B. The athletics association ran out of money
C. The chancellor deemed the sport too dangerous

---

11. B — The *Clarion-Ledger* reported that most spectators jumped the gate and refused to pay
12. A
13. B
14. A
15. A

16. An 1897 contest was held to name the university's annual. The winner: Ole Miss. From where was the term "Ole Miss" derived?
A. Ole Man River
B. It was a term slaves used to refer to the wife of the plantation owner.
C. Slang for Old Mississippi

17. In naming the first annual, "Ole Miss" was submitted late in the process by Elma Meek of Oxford. What was the leading submission prior to Miss Meek's suggestion?
A. The Old Master
B. The Cotton Boll
C. The Republican

18. During the four active seasons between 1893-1897, the university football squad (or their opponents) scored a total of four points in four different games. Why was four points such a typical final score during that period?
A. Safeties were much more common in the early days
B. An incomplete pass cost a team 2 points
C. A touchdown was worth four points

19. In 1898 what were Ole Miss players encouraged to do to protect themselves?
A. Wear pads
B. Grow their hair long
C. Wear multiple layers of clothing

20. In 1898, who made his first appearance at an Ole Miss football game?
A. The Governor of Mississippi
B. William Faulkner
C. Blind Jim Ivy

---

16. B
17. B
18. C
19. B
20. C

21. Jim Bell, the founding dean of the Ole Miss School of Commerce, was a member of the 1898 team. What was his nickname?
A. Handlebar
B. Uncle
C. Big Boy

22. Hugh White, who was later elected governor of Mississippi, was a member of the 1898 and 1899 Ole Miss team. What was White's nickname?
A. Mad Dog
B. Shrimp
C. Fatty

23. What was the record of the 1900 Ole Miss team?
A. 3-0
B. 0-3
C. 2-1

24. In what year did Ole Miss win its first game over Mississippi A&M?
A. 1902
B. 1900
C. 1920

25. In 1902 the Ole Miss team did not wear helmets. Instead, some players opted to wear what kind of equipment?
A. Nose guards
B. Sunglasses
C. Chin guards

26. In 1904, Ole Miss suffered a staggering defeat against Vanderbilt. What was the score?
A. 40-0
B. 69-0
C. 97-0

---

21. B
22. C
23. B
24. A
25. A
26. B

27. Two weeks after the Vanderbilt defeat, Ole Miss scored a record-setting number of points in a single game against Southwest Baptist University. What was the score?
A. 90-5
B. 70-2
C. 114-0

28. Ole Miss endured one season without a score. What year was that?
A. 1903
B. 1905
C. 1907

29. The 1905 Ole Miss team was dismal; however, they did contribute to football history. How?
A. They donated footballs to every high school in Mississippi
B. They helped form the Southeastern Conference
C. They taught the game to youngsters who would play the first high school game in the state

30. In what year did Ole Miss throw its first legal forward pass?
A. 1905
B. 1906
C. 1907

31. The 1907 Ole Miss football coach, Frank Mason, encouraged his players to punch opponents when the referee wasn't looking (a practice he started as a player at Harvard in 1892). What was Coach Mason's nickname?
A. Slugger
B. Boxer
C. Fightin' Frank

---

27. C
28. B
29. C
30. B
31. A

32. What was the win/loss record for the 1907 Ole Miss team?
A. 0-6
B. 1-5
C. 2-4

33. Opponents scored 195 points against Ole Miss in 1907. How many points did Ole Miss score during the 1907 season?
A. 6
B. 12
C. 21

34: In order to keep the Ole Miss players warm during the 1907 game against Mississippi A&M, what did "Slugger" Mason give his players to drink in the second half?
A. Whiskey
B. Coffee
C. Cider

35. The Bleacher Report ranked the 1907 Ole Miss squad as one of the worst in the history of football. What place did the 1907 team hold?
A. The worst
B. The second worst
C. The third worst

36. What was the record of the 1910 Ole Miss squad?
A. 0-8
B. 6-2
C. 7-1

---

32. A
33. A — against Missouri Normal College
34. A
35. B — the 1922 Arkansas State squad was voted the worst ever
36. C

37. Of the victories in 1910, how many were shutouts?
A. 5
B. 7
C. None

38. The 1910 defense held opponents to how many points per game?
A. 5.11
B. 3.17
C. 1.12

39. The 1911 Ole Miss-Mississippi A&M game is notable because . . .
A. It was the first game played on Thanksgiving day
B. The grandstands collapsed
C. A tornado hit during halftime

40. Following the 1911 season, the faculty suspended five star football players. What was the reason for the suspension?
A. Fighting
B. Rigging a game
C. Professionalism

41. In 1913, the selection for the location of the new football field was made by an Ole Miss coach (it is where Vaught-Hemingway is located today). Name the coach.
A. Billy Driver
B. Dudy Noble
C. Nathan Stauffer

42. November 27, 1913, was an unusual day in Ole Miss football history. Why?
A. The team, in protest of faculty policy, walked off the field at halftime
B. Two Ole Miss teams played games in different states
C. The team changed colors, for this one day, to purple and gold

---

37. B
38. C — Only Vandy scored against the 1910 team.
39. B
40. C
41. A
42. B

43. In what year did Ole Miss play its first game in the stadium that is now known as Vaught-Hemingway?
A. 1947
B. 1930
C. 1914

44. Who was the first Ole Miss player to score a touchdown in the brand new stadium?
A. Charlie Conerly
B. Tad Smith
C. W.C. Dear

45. The first time the Ole Miss football team wore numbered jerseys was in a game against LSU. What year did this happen?
A. 1895
B. 1914
C. 1921

46. On October 4, 1915, what celebration took place?
A. The first Homecoming game
B. The first home game featuring a band
C. "Blind Jim" Ivy's wedding

47. On October 23, 1915, Ole Miss suffered its worst loss (0-91) in history. To what team did we lose?
A. Tulane
B. Vanderbilt
C. Sewanee

---

43. C
44. C
45. B
46. C
47. B

48. Coach C.R. "Dudy" Noble (1917-1918) had a terrible run as head coach at Ole Miss. Which of the following statements is true?
A. He holds the distinction as the only coach to lose to Mississippi A&M *twice* in the same year
B. He told a reporter: "I know what hell is like because I coached at Ole Miss"
C. He named a lazy, mutt dog that wouldn't hunt "Ole Miss"
D. All of the above

49. In 1920, three star football players were expelled from Ole Miss. Why?
A. Poor grades
B. Refusing to cut their hair
C. Protesting a ban on dances

50. In 1920, Governor Lee Russell ordered all Ole Miss students (including football players) to sign a pledge that they would not join a Greek fraternity and that they would not participate in dances that "contributed to the moral decay" of college students. What happened three years later to Governor Russell?
A. Elected Bishop of the Episcopal Church
B. Sued for seduction by his former stenographer, but later acquitted.
C. Elected to the U.S. Congress

51. In December 1921, the Ole Miss team set sail to play a game on what island?
A. Cuba
B. Hawaii
C. Antigua

---

48. D
49. C
50. B
51. A

52. During a game against the Cuban Athletic Club in Havana (which Ole Miss lost 0-14), how many Ole Miss touchdowns were called back due to "penalties?"
A. 0
B. 5
C. 3

---

52. C

THE MODERN ERA

1. In 1925, Ole Miss hired its first football coach with a star pedigree. What was his name?
A. Homer Hazel
B. Ed Walker
C. Harry Mehre

2. This coach was a star at what school?
A. Notre Dame
B. Rutgers
C. Harvard

3. What was his most notable achievement as a player?
A. He scored nine touchdowns in a single game
B. He was the first two-time All-American at two different positions
C. He broke records set by Jim Thorpe

4. What was Homer Hazel's top salary?
A. $2,000
B. $3,100
C. $8,000

5. When Homer Hazel was hired by Ole Miss, what goal did the athletics association set out for him?
A. Win a Southern Conference championship
B. Beat Mississippi A&M
C. Defeat mighty Vanderbilt

---

1. A
2. B
3. B
4. C
5. B

6. Homer Hazel's first All-Southern Conference player was a fullback from Rolling Fork, Mississippi. What was his name?
A. C.M. "Tad" Smith
B. Solly Cohen
C. Thad "Pie" Vann

7. In 1926, Ole Miss broke a 13-game losing streak against Mississippi A&M. After that game, the students at both schools purchased a trophy to be held annually by the winning school. What prompted the "egg" trophy?
A. Student body presidents at each school who had been childhood friends
B. A riot after the 1926 game
C. The introduction of cheerleaders at both schools

8. What year did Ole Miss and Mississippi State create the Golden Egg trophy?
A. 1902
B. 1913
C. 1927

9. In what year was an early rendition of Hotty Toddy introduced at Ole Miss?
A. 1926
B. 1927
C. 1929

10. One of the early stars of Ole Miss football was C.M. "Tad" Smith. Which of the following statements is true?
A. He never wore a helmet
B. He never called a fair catch when returning a punt
C. He taped his ears back to prevent wind resistance
D. All of the above

---

6. B
7. B
8. C
9. A
10. D

11. Since the early days, the football team had been called "the Red and Blue" or "the University Boys" or "the Mighty Mississippians." In 1929, Ole Miss selected its first official nickname. What was it?
A. Rebels
B. Flood
C. Democrats

12. In 1930, a new coach, Ed Walker, was hired by Ole Miss. Who was Walker's mentor?
A. Jim Thorpe
B. Pop Warner
C. Knute Rockne

13. In 1932, for the first time, two Ole Miss players were selected to play in the North-South All-Star Game. Those two players were . . .
A. Ray Hapes and Bruiser Kinard
B. Tom Swayze and Guy Turnbow
C. Merle Hapes and Junie Hovious

14. In 1932, Ole Miss joined what conference?
A. SIAA (Southern Intercollegiate Athletic Association)
B. Southern Conference
C. The Southeastern Conference

15. In 1935, Ole Miss received its first invitation to a major post-season bowl. What bowl was it?
A. Sugar
B. Orange
C. Rose

---

11. B
12. B
13. B
14. C
15. B

16. In 1936, Ole Miss student and *Mississippian* sports editor Billy Gates held a contest to replace the nickname "Flood" with another, more suitable nickname. "Rebels" was selected as the new nickname by a vote of 4-3. What came in second place?
A. Raiders
B. Stonewalls
C. Ole Miss

17. Who was the first Ole Miss player selected as an All-American?
A. Buster Poole
B. Bruiser Kinard
C. Ray Hapes

18. Who was the first Ole Miss player selected in the NFL draft in 1937?
A. Buster Poole
B. Bruiser Kinard
C. Ray Hapes

19. In 1937, Ole Miss was the first team to fly en masse to a college football game. What team did Ole Miss play?
A. Villanova
B. Temple
C. Penn

20. In 1938, Harry Mehre was hired to be the head coach at Ole Miss. From what college did we hire away Mehre?
A. Auburn
B. Alabama
C. Georgia

---

16. C
17. B
18. A
19. B
20. C

21. Harry Mehre played center from 1919-1921 for what famous college coach?
A. Pop Warner
B. Knute Rockne
C. John Heisman

22. In 1920, one of Mehre's Notre Dame teammates told him he had "a sore throat." On his deathbed, this player inspired a famous movie scene. What was Mehre's teammate's name?
A. George Gipp
B. Paul Hornung
C. George O'Connor

23. In Mehre's first four seasons, he never . . .
A. Lost to Mississippi State
B. Lost more than two games
C. Lost a game by more than five points

24. During Mehre's first season, his star player was Tunica native Parker Hall. Hall led the nation in how many individual record categories?
A. 2
B. 6
C. 10

25. The 1939 team lost its star player, Jesse Ward, who could have had an All-American career. What happened?
A. He was drafted
B. He was expelled from school
C. He died in an automobile accident

---

21. B
22. A
23. B
24. B
25. C

26. In 1938, Mehre met a 135-pound recruit who would become an Ole Miss star. Mehre discounted the young man and said, "If I have to play boys that size, I may as well go back to Georgia." Who was the recruit?
A. Junie Hovious
B. Merle Hapes
C. Charlie Conerly

27. Before the United States entered World War II, Harry Mehre had the highest winning percentage of any coach in Ole Miss history.
A. True
B. False

28. In 1943, Ole Miss didn't field a football team. Mehre, who couldn't serve in the war due to problems with eyesight, hired Moss Point native Eddie Khayat in 1943 to perform what task?
A. Train students in hand-to-hand combat
B. Train students in leadership
C. Train students in the manufacturing of arms
D. All of the above

29. In 1945, despite student protests, Harry Mehre was fired. Harold "Red" Drew was hired to replace him. From what school did Ole Miss hire Drew?
A. LSU
B. Auburn
C. Alabama

30. As an assistant coach at Alabama in the 1930s, Drew coached offensive ends. His most famous receiver was the incomparable Don Hutson. Who was his second most notable end at Alabama?
A. John Vaught
B. Paul "Bear" Bryant
C. Robert Neyland

---

26. A
27. A
28. A
29. C
30. B

31. Harold "Red" Drew spent one year as head coach at Ole Miss. But he hired a young offensive line coach named John Vaught. For what program did Vaught coach before coming to Ole Miss?
A. SMU
B. TCU
C. North Carolina preflight

---

31. C

VAUGHT ERA

1. Harold "Red" Drew was hired in 1946. How many years did he coach for Ole Miss?
A. 5
B. 1
C. 12

2. What was Ole Miss record during the 1946 season under head coach Harold Drew?
A. 4-5
B. 5-4
C. 2-7

3. The Rebels faced a number of problems, post-war, during the 1946 football season. One of those problems was that the team's jerseys did not arrive in time for the first game. Whose hand-me-down jerseys did the Ole Miss players wear in the first game?
A. Alabama's
B. LSU's
C. Mississippi State's

4. There are only two players to get a lifetime ban from playing in the NFL, one of them is Frank Filchock, the other is an Ole Miss player. Who was the Ole Miss player banned?
A. Ray Hapes
B. Buster Poole
C. Merle Hapes

---

1. B
2. C
3. A
4. C — Hapes was banned for considering a payoff to throw the NFL Championship game in 1946.

5. John Vaught agreed to be the Ole Miss head coach on one condition: if a particular player returned to play in the 1947 season. Who was that player?
A. Barney Poole
B. Charlie Conerly
C. Kayo Dottley

6. Before the start of the great 1947 season, Coach Vaught accepted a bid to a postseason bowl game. What bowl game was this?
A. Delta Bowl
B. Orange Bowl
C. Rose Bowl

7. Coach Vaught's first game as head coach of the Ole Miss team was a win against Kentucky. Who was the head coach of Kentucky?
A. Robert Neyland
B. Paul "Bear" Byrant
C. Ralph Jordan

8. John Vaught played defensive tackle in college for what team?
A. Texas A&M
B. Texas Christian University
C. University of Texas

9. What was Vaught's best record at Ole Miss?
A. 10-0
B. 12-0
C. 9-1

10. In how many Bowl games did Ole Miss play under head coach John Vaught?
A. 12
B. 20
C. 18

---

5. B
6. A
7. B
8. B
9. A
10. C

11. John Vaught holds the Ole Miss record for most shutout victories in his career as a head coach. How many shutout victories did his teams win?
A. 64
B. 34
C. 42

12. How many first-team All-Americans came out of the Vaught era at Ole Miss?
A. 56
B. 30
C. 12

13. How many players were drafted into the professional ranks of football from the Vaught era at Ole Miss?
A. 120
B. 176
C. 84

14. Ole Miss quarterback Charlie Conerly had two distinct nicknames. Which one of these is not one of these two nicknames?
A. Cowboy Killer
B. Roach
C. Chuckin Charlie

15. How did Charlie Conerly get his nickname Roach?
A. Selling roaches to fisherman during the Great Depression
B. Playing for the Clarksdale Roaches
C. Scurrying around the baseball bases fast, resembling a roach

---

11. A
12. B
13. B
14. A
15. C

16. Along with football Charlie Conerly was a superb athlete in what other college sport?
A. Baseball
B. Basketball
C. Ice Hockey

17. Charlie Conerly led Ole Miss to a victory over LSU in 1947, but a late-game interception almost cost the Rebels the game. LSU defensive back Y.A. Tittle intercepted a pass and almost scored a touchdown to win, if not for one fluke. What happened to Tittle?
A. He tripped over a shoe
B. His pants fell down
C. He fumbled the ball while waving to a fan

18. In 1945 Conerly was drafted to the NFL by the Washington Redskins, who later traded his rights to the New York Giants. In his first season with the Giants (1948), what award did he win?
A. The Conerly Trophy
B. NFL Rookie of the Year
C. The Walter Payton Award

19. Charlie Conerly's New York Giants won the NFL championship game in what year?
A. 1956
B. 1960
C. 1959

20. What year was Ole Miss's first SEC title, as well as first bowl game victory?
A. 1936
B. 1947
C. 1983

---

16. A
17. B
18. B
19. A
20. B

21. In the 1948 season, the Ole Miss wide receiver Barney Poole was hit so intensely by a defender that he broke his jaw. How many teeth did he lose?
A. 8
B. 4
C. 0

22. In the 1949 season, the Rebels suffered their only losing season during the John Vaught era, but one Ole Miss player won the national rushing title. Who?
A. Arnold Boykin
B. Jimmy Lear
C. Kayo Dottley

23. For how many yards did Kayo Dottley rush in 1949?
A. 1,001 yards
B. 1,543 yards
C. 1,312 yards

24. In 1949, Kayo Dottley also broke a national record for rushes in a single game versus Mississippi State on November 26, 1949. How many times did Dottley run the ball?
A. 30
B. 35
C. 40

25. Where did John Dottley's nickname "Kayo" originate?
A. The boxing term "K.O."
B. A koala bear
C. The opposite of "Okay"

---

21. A
22. C
23. C
24. C
25. A

26. Who was the first Ole Miss running back to have back-to-back 1,000-yard rushing seasons?
A. Deuce McCalister
B. Kayo Dottley
C. Arnold "Showboat" Boykin

27. How many Ole Miss records and SEC records did Kayo Dottley hold at the end of his college career at Ole Miss?
A. Six Ole Miss records and two SEC records
B. Nine Ole Miss records and three SEC records
C. Seven Ole Miss records and one SEC record

28. How many Ole Miss records does Kayo Dottley hold 69 years after his last game?
A. Three
B. Two
C. Five

29. Going into the 1951 season coach Vaught set new rules for the Ole Miss football team. Which one of these was *not* a new rule set by Coach Vaught that year?
A. No signing married players
B. Players can't have cars during the football season
C. Players could not drink alcohol
D. Players couldn't visit home during the football season
E. Players had to walk to class and practice

30. In the 1951 game against Mississippi State, Arnold "Showboat" Boykin scored an NCAA record number of rushing touchdowns in a single game. How many touchdowns did he score?
A. 7
B. 5
C. 10

---

26. B
27. B
28. A
29. C
30. A

31. For how many years did that NCAA record stand?
A. 10
B. 19
C. 39

32. Which Ole Miss player scored the most points in a game?
A. AJ Brown
B. Eli Manning
C. Showboat Boykin

33. During the 1952 season, Ole Miss defeated a team that had the No. 1 ranked defense in the nation. Many believe this Ole Miss victory put the Rebels into the national spotlight for the first time. What team did the Rebels beat?
A. Harvard
B. Alabama
C. Maryland

34. What was the first year in which the Rebels lost no regular-season games?
A. 1947
B. 1952
C. 1961

35. Jimmy Lear was an All-American quarterback at Ole Miss, but he also lettered in many other sports. Which of these sports did Lear *not* play?
A. Baseball
B. Track
C. Tennis
D. Golf

---

31. C
32. C
33. C
34. B
35. C

36. Who caught the first touchdown pass in the 1952 Ole Miss upset over Maryland game?
A. Ray "Buck" Howell
B. Bud Slay
C. Bud Howell

37. When did Ole Miss first play in the Sugar Bowl?
A. January 1, 1953
B. January 1, 1951
C. January 1, 1947

38. In 1954 the Ole Miss football team traveled to Philadelphia to face off against Villanova. The Rebels won in front of the biggest crowd to attend a college football game that season — 95,607 people. What was the final score of the game?
A. 24-21
B. 10-3
C. 52-0

39. In 1956 Ole Miss won its first Cotton Bowl game in a hard-fought battle that ended with a score of 14-13. What team did Ole Miss face? (Hint: it is the alma mater of John Vaught)
A. Texas Chrisitan University
B. Mississippi State
C. Florida

40. Ole Miss has won back-to-back SEC championships twice in the school's long-standing football history. What were the first years?
A. 1954-1955
B. 1947-1948
C. 1903-1904

---

36. A
37. A
38. C
39. A
40. A

41. Kayo Dottley was selected in the second round of the NFL draft, but a freak accident would cut his pro career short. What team drafted Dottley?
A. Green Bay Packers
B. Chicago Bears
C. Detroit Lions

42. In the early days of Vaught's coaching career, almost no players lifted weights. Vaught wanted "country strong" men. When one player insisted on weights, what did coach Vaught provide?
A. Coffee cans filled with concrete stuck together by an iron rod
B. Railroad Ties
C. Rocks

43. What was Vaught's go-to work out when training the Ole Miss football team?
A. Jumping Jacks
B. Pull-ups
C. Sprints

44. Herman Sidney Day was a great Ole Miss quarterback, but he may be better known by his nickname "Eagle" Day. The press gave Day a second nickname. What was it?
A. Trout
B. The Mississippi Gambler
C. Soaring E

45. What did Day do to earn this nickname?
A. He was gambling on the game beforehand
B. He faked a field goal and instead scrambled for a late-game touchdown.
C. He ignored coach Vaught's instructions to punt and instead he threw a 13-yard pass to fullback Paige Cothren.

---

41. B
42. A
43. C
44. B
45. C

46. Which Ole Miss player won the Most Valuable Player award at the 1956 Cotton Bowl?
A. Eagle Day
B. Kayo Dottley
C. Billy Ray Adams

47. During Coach Vaught's career at Ole Miss, one coach was designated to scout every Mississippi State game. Who was this Ole Miss coach?
A. Bonnie "Country" Graham
B. Junie Hovious
C. Wobble Davidson

48. What was Vaught's record against in-state rival Mississippi State?
A. 25-0
B. 19-2-4
C. 16-6-3

49. Charlie Conerly won the NFL Most Valuable Player award in what year?
A. 1962
B. 1954
C. 1959

50. During the 1958 NFL season, a former Ole Miss defensive back led the league with 11 interceptions. He ended his career with a total of 52 interceptions. Who was it?
A. Larry Grantham
B. Jimmy Patton
C. Jackie Simpson

---

46. A
47. A
48. B
49. C
50. B

51. The 1959 Ole Miss team is one of the greatest NCAA teams in football history, with the defense dominating opponents. How many shutout victories did the Rebels have in the 1959 season?
A. eight
B. two
C. four

52. Who was the captain of the historic 1959 football team?
A. Eagle Day
B. Jake Gibbs
C. Charlie Flowers

53. On October 31, 1959, #3 Ole Miss played #1 LSU. LSU won 7-3. The Tigers scored on a fluke, 89-yard punt return. Who scored the touchdown?
A. Warren Rabb
B. Johnny Robinson
C. Billy Cannon

54. During the 1959 season, the Ole Miss offense racked up a total of 329 points. How many points were scored by opponents of Ole Miss in 1959?
A. 52
B. 21
C. 0

55. One of the notable Vaught-era linebackers, Larry Grantham, played 13 seasons in the AFL and helped the New York Jets win Super Bowl III. How many times during Grantham's career did he miss a game?
A. 3
B. 12
C. 10

---

51. A
52. C
53. C
54. B
55. A

56. During the 1958 and 1959 seasons, an Ole Miss kicker led the nation in kick scoring. Who was this outstanding kicker?
A. Bobby Ray Franklin
B. Paige Cothren
C. Robert Khayat

57. In 1960, for the first time, a Rebel athlete was named an All-American in two different sports, football and baseball. Who was this player?
A. Jake Gibbs
B. Eagle Day
C. Jimmy Lear

58. Jake Gibbs finished third in the 1960 Heisman voting, but after the school year ended, he decided to play professional baseball. What baseball team signed Gibbs?
A. The Saint Louis Cardinals
B. The New York Yankees
C. The Los Angeles Dodgers

59. In 1960, Jake Gibbs's signing bonus was the largest in club history. How much was his signing bonus?
A. $50,000
B. $80,000
C. $100,000

60. Ole Miss lost the 1962 Cotton Bowl to Texas. A star player suffered a career-ending automobile accident the week before the bowl. Who was the player?
A. Louis Guy
B. Art Doty
C. Billy Ray Adams

---

56. C
57. A
58. B
59. C
60. C

61. Billy Ray Adams had one carry for a loss in his entire football career. Against what team did Adams lose yardage on a rushing play?
A. Tulane
B. Auburn
C. Vanderbilt

62. In the 1962 game against Tennessee, Ole Miss was at risk of ruining an undefeated season. An Ole Miss player saved the day by intercepting a pass and returning it 103 yards for a touchdown. Who was the player?
A. Fred Roberts
B. A.J. Holloway
C. Louis Guy

63. Louis Guy's interception tied the Ole Miss record for the longest interception return. Who set the initial record?
A. Ray Hapes
B. Merle Hapes
C. Junie Hovious

64. Jim Weatherly's botched play during 1962 Egg Bowl resulted in an Ole Miss touchdown. What play was called when Weatherly missed the handoff?
A. QB option
B. HB dive
C. 35 trap

65. Ole Miss had one perfect season (no losses; no ties). What year was it?
A. 1959
B. 1962
C. 1960

---

61. A
62. C
63. A
64. C
65. B

66. Jim Weatherly finished his Ole Miss career second to Charlie Conerly in school passing records. Weatherly passed on a professional football career. What did Weatherly pursue?
A. Astronaut
B. Mechanical engineer
C. Songwriting

67. John Vaught generally got what he wanted. However, he could not convince one remarkable Ole Miss athlete (an All-American player in basketball and baseball who was also an All-American quarterback on his high school team) to play football for the Rebels. Who was that Ole Miss athlete?
A. Don Kessinger
B. Dan Jordan
C. Alfred Nichols

68. In 1966, Ole Miss signed one of the greatest college quarterbacks in NCAA history. Who was this quarterback?
A. Archie Manning
B. Jake Gibbs
C. Glynn Griffing

69. During his freshman year at Ole Miss, Archie Manning played quarterback on the freshman squad, but he was required to play defense during two games as well. What was Manning's defensive position?
A. Outside linebacker
B. Cornerback
C. Safety

70. Archie Manning's high school coach, Gerald Morgan, encouraged him to pursue what sport to improve his football skills?
A. Handball
B. Baseball
C. Track

---

66. C
67. A
68. A
69. C
70. C

71. Which Ole Miss staff member was primarily responsible for recruiting Archie Manning?
A. John Vaught
B. Roy Stinnett
C. Wobble Davidson

72. Who was the Rebel freshman coach during most of the Vaught era?
A. Wobble Davidson
B. Bob Tyler
C. Bruiser Kinard

73. What was the one priority Coach Davidson instilled in every freshman player before they joined the varsity squad?
A. How to tackle
B. How to stay hydrated
C. How to catch the ball

74. What year did "Archie Fever" begin?
A. 1968
B. 1969
C. 1970

75. What band recorded the song *The Ballad of Archie Who*?
A. Crosby Stills and Nash
B. The Rebel Rousers
C. Elvis Presley

---

71. B
72. A
73. A
74. B
75. B

76. In a historic college football game on October 4, 1969, Ole Miss played against Alabama on primetime television. It was the first college football game broadcast during primetime by a major network. What network aired the game?
A. CBS
B. ABC
C. NBC

77. Ole Miss lost the first primetime televised game against Alabama in a well-fought offensive battle. What was the final score of the game?
A. 10-7
B. 20-21
C. 33-32

78. On October 11, 1969, Cloyce Hinton set an Ole Miss record for the longest field goal in a game against Georgia. How long was the kick?
A. 52 yards
B. 55 yards
C. 59 yards

79. In the 1970 season, Ole Miss lost star quarterback Archie Manning to injury. Who were the Rebels playing?
A. Houston
B. Tulane
C. Arkansas

80. Even with a broken arm Archie Manning played in the 1971 Gator Bowl. The Rebels lost 35-28 to what team?
A. Tennessee
B. Florida
C. Auburn

---

76. B
77. C
78. C — At the time it was an NCAA record.
79. A
80. C

81. In the 1971 Gator Bowl, with his left arm in a cast, Archie Manning gained how many total yards?
A. 275
B. 180
C. 210

82. During the 1970 season, John Vaught was forced to relinquish the head coaching duties. Why?
A. Major circulatory problems with his heart
B. He suffered a stroke
C. A broken leg

83. Who filled John Vaught's role during the remainder of the 1970 season?
A. Billy Kinard
B. Bruiser Kinard
C. Junie Hovious

84. Archie Manning's number 18 jersey has been retired at Ole Miss. The university celebrates his football legacy another way. How so?
A. The maximum classroom size at the honors college is 18
B. The speed limit in some areas is 18 mph
C. A full-size bronze statue of Archie Manning

85. Paul "Bear" Bryant said of one Ole Miss player, "The best college quarterback I've ever seen." Who was Bryant talking about?
A. Jimmy Lear
B. Charlie Conerly
C. Archie Manning

---

81. A
82. A
83. B
84. B
85. C

86. An Ole Miss player holds the SEC record for 37 career sacks. He also holds the single-season mark with 18. Who is this player?
A. Ben Williams
B. Larry Grantham
C. Patrick Willis

87. Who was the first African American to play on the Ole Miss varsity team?
A. Patrick Willis
B. Ben Williams
C. Deuce Mcallister

88. Ben Williams was the first African American to play on the varsity football team at Ole Miss, but there was another player who broke boundaries alongside him. What minority player also came to Ole Miss in 1972 but played on the freshman team?
A. James Storey
B. Buford McGee
C. James Reed

89. In 1975 an Ole Miss football player won the title "Colonel Reb" (now called Mr. Ole Miss) — an award voted on by the students that is similar to a homecoming king award. Who was named Colonel Rebel in 1975?
A. Tim Ellis
B. Archie Manning
C. Ben Williams

90. For a campus stunt in 1975, Ben Williams wrestled an animal during a Rebel basketball game. What animal did he wrestle?
A. A bear
B. A python
C. A kangaroo

---

86. A
87. B
88. C
89. C
90. A

91. After the 1970 season, Coach John Vaught officially stepped down as head coach at Ole Miss. How many years did he lead Ole Miss?
A. 20 years
B. 32 years
C. 24 years

92. How many SEC titles did Coach Vaught win during his illustrious career?
A. 6
B. 5
C. 4

93. Who was named the head coach after Vaught's retirement?
A. Steve Sloan
B. Billy Kinard
C. Ken Cooper

94. Vaught had handpicked a coach to succeed him, but he was passed over by the selection committee. Who was the coach?
A. Bob Tyler
B. Ken Cooper
C. Bruiser Kinard

95. In the first season under Billy Kinard Ole Miss finished with a record of 10-2. What teams defeated the Rebels?
A. Alabama and Arkansas
B. Georgia and Alabama
C. Texas and LSU

---

91. C — plus the final eight games in 1973 after Billy Kinard was fired
92. A
93. B
94. A
95. B

96. In the 1971 season, Ole Miss defeated Georgia Tech in the Peach Bowl. What was the final score?
A. 41-18
B. 28-10
C. 34-28

97. Billy Kinard's Ole Miss coaching career didn't last long. His record, along with his abrasive personality, led to his dismissal after the third game of the 1973 season. Who replaced Kinard mid-season?
A. Ken Cooper
B. Steve Sloan
C. John Vaught

98. John Vaught's last game as Rebel head coach was a victory against Mississippi State on November 24, 1973. What was the score?
A. 7-6
B. 21-0
C. 38-10

---

96. A
97. C
98. C

COOPER AND SLOAN ERA

1. Who hired Ken Cooper as an assistant coach?
A. John Vaught
B. Billy Kinard
C. Billy Brewer

2. What was Ken Cooper's first-season record with Ole Miss?
A. 3-8
B. 5-6
C. 7-4

3. Which season did Ken Cooper win SEC Coach of the Year?
A. 1974
B. 1977
C. 1975

4. What was Ken Cooper's SEC record when he won SEC Coach of the Year?
A. 5-1
B. 6-0
C. 4-2

5. Which SEC team beat Ole Miss in the 1975 season?
A. Auburn
B. Alabama
C. LSU

6. What was Ken Cooper's best season record during his Ole Miss career?
A. 6-5
B. 3-8
C. 9-2

---

1. B
2. A
3. C
4. A
5. B
6. A

7. Under Ken Cooper, Ole Miss shocked the world in 1977 by defeating a number-three nationally-ranked team. This team would go on to win the national championship in 1977. Name the school.
A. Alabama
B. Notre Dame
C. USC

8. One player made 17 tackles against the Fighting Irish. Who was this player?
A. Ben Williams
B. George Plasketes
C. Charlie Cage

9. Ole Miss played two quarterbacks during the Notre Dame game; which one of these quarterbacks didn't play in the game?
A. Jim Lear
B. Tim Ellis
C. Bobby Garner

10. Who was Notre Dame's future All-American quarterback who sat on the bench and watched his team lose to Ole Miss?
A. Joe Namath
B. Joe Montana
C. Joe Theismann

11. What did the Fighting Irish use to try to stay cool during the blistering hot Mississippi day?
A. Blocks of ice
B. Wet towels
C. Mini fans

---

7. B
8. C
9. A
10. B
11. A

12. Who caught the go-ahead touchdown pass from Ellis that gave Ole Miss the lead in the 1977 game against Notre Dame?
A. Leon Perry
B. L.Q. Smith
C. James Storey

13. What was the final score of the Ole Miss vs. Notre Dame game in 1977?
A. 14-7
B. 20-13
C. 42-35

14. What position did Ken Cooper play in college?
A. Wide receiver
B. Kicker
C. Defensive end

15. For what college did Ken Cooper play football?
A. Georgia
B. Ole Miss
C. Tulane

16. Where did Ken Cooper start his coaching career?
A. Ole Miss
B. Georgia
C. Texas

17. Ken Cooper stepped away from coaching football in 1977. He became an executive at what corporation?
A. Bell South
B. Nike
C. State Farm Insurance

---

12. C
13. B
14. C
15. A
16. B
17. A

18. Which coach was hired in 1978 to replace Ken Cooper?
A. Billy Brewer
B. Steve Sloan
C. Tommy Tuberville

19. How would Steve Sloan motivate the Ole Miss football players?
A. Bible verses
B. Screaming
C. Wild chants before games

20. Which defensive coach helped Sloan at Vanderbilt and Texas Tech but did not come to Ole Miss?
A. Ray Perkins
B. Bill Parcells
C. Jim Carmody

21. Where did Steve Sloan play college football?
A. Alabama
B. Texas Tech
C. Vanderbilt

22. What famous quarterback did Steve Sloan back up at Alabama?
A. Scott Hunter
B. Ken Stabler
C. Joe Namath

23. How many SEC titles did Alabama win while Steve Sloan was their starting quarterback?
A. 0
B. 1
C. 2

---

18. B
19. A
20. B
21. A
22. C
23. C

24. What was Sloan's best season record during his Ole Miss career?
A. 5-6
B. 7-4
C. 9-2

25. In 1982, Ole Miss finished with a record of 4-7. What was the team's record in SEC play?
A. 4-2
B. 0-6
C. 3-3

26. Steve Sloan left Ole Miss at the end of the 1982 season. At what school did he accept the head coaching position?
A. Duke
B. Clemson
C. Auburn

27. Who was Steve Sloan's mentor?
A. Joe Namath
B. Paul "Bear" Bryant
C. Ray Perkins

---

24. A
25. B
26. A
27. B

BREWER ERA

1. Billy Brewer was the head coach at what university in Louisiana when he was named head coach at Ole Miss in December 1982?
A. Southeastern Louisiana
B. McNeese State
C. Louisiana Tech

2. Billy Brewer's first victory as the Ole Miss head coach was in 1983 against what team and head coach?
A. Memphis State and Rex Dockery
B. Arkansas and Lou Holtz
C. Alabama and Ray Perkins

3. In Billy Brewer's first season as head coach in 1983, Ole Miss finished the regular season with a 6-5 on the field record. What was the team's record after six games?
A. 1-5
B. 2-4
C. 3-3

4. After beating Mississippi State 24-23 to end the 1983 regular season, Ole Miss played Air Force in what bowl game?
A. Independence
B. Liberty
C. Gator

5. Which Ole Miss quarterback led the Rebels to victories against Vanderbilt, LSU, Tennessee, and Mississippi State to end the 1983 regular season?
A. John Fourcade
B. Kent Austin
C. Kelly Powell

---

1. C
2. B
3. A
4. A
5. C

6. After the 1983 season, an Ole Miss loss to what team was reversed to a win due to this team's playing a quarterback ruled ineligible by the NCAA, giving the Rebels seven regular season victories in Billy Brewer's first year as head coach?
A. Alabama
B. Southern Mississippi
C. Tulane

7. Who was the placekicker for the 1983 Ole Miss team in Billy Brewer's first season as head coach?
A. Neil Teevan
B. Todd Gatlin
C. Brian Lee

8. Who led the 1983 Rebels in rushing with 580 yards and seven touchdowns?
A. Nathan Wonsley
B. Buford McGee
C. Arthur Humphrey

9. Who had the most touchdown receptions (three) on the 1983 Rebel squad?
A. Tim Moffett
B. Buford McGee
C. Jamie Holder

10. What 1983 Ole Miss victory is known as "The Immaculate Deflection" game with the opposition's missing a short field goal in the last seconds, the result of a strong wind gust?
A. Mississippi State
B. LSU
C. Tennessee

---

6. C
7. A
8. B
9. A
10. A

11. On October 8, 1983, Billy Brewer rekindled a dormant Ole Miss tradition by leading his players on a walk through the Grove on their way to the stadium as fans stood along the sidewalk and cheered. Who was the opponent that day?
A. Alabama
B. Arkansas
C. Georgia

12. Who did Ole Miss beat 19-14 on Homecoming Day in Oxford in 1984?
A. Tulane
B. Vanderbilt
C. Georgia

13. What name was given the eclectic collection of writers, teachers, townsfolk, and their often famous guests who achieved significant prominence as super fans during the Coach Billy Brewer era?
A. The Bleacher Bums
B. The South End Zone Rowdies
C. The Hoity Toity Hecklers

14. In 1984 Ole Miss won its second consecutive Egg Bowl, defeating MSU by what score?
A. 24-3
B. 24-23
C. 45-0

15. This future All-American, College Football Hall of Famer, and NFL great played defensive end beginning in 1985, but before his college career ended four seasons later, also starred at tight end.
A. Kris Mangum
B. Wesley Walls
C. Doug Zeigler

---

11. C
12. A
13. B
14. A
15. B

16. Billy Brewer's first eight Rebel squads dominated Mississippi State. What was his team's record against the Bulldogs from 1983-90?
A. 7-1
B. 6-2
C. 6-1-1

17. Ole Miss hadn't won on this opponent's field since 1968 when the Rebels claimed a thrilling victory there in 1986.
A. Bryant-Denny Stadium at Alabama
B. Tiger Stadium at LSU
C. Sanford Stadium at Georgia

18. The Rebels won 20-17 against this opponent in the 1986 Independence Bowl.
A. Oklahoma
B. Oklahoma State
C. Texas Tech

19. Which quarterback passed for an Ole Miss record of 343 yards in the 1986 Independence Bowl victory?
A. Mark Young
B. Kent Austin
C. John Darnell

20. Multi-talented defensive player Tony Bennett lettered four seasons beginning in 1986. What was his nickname?
A. Bear
B. Snake
C. Gator

---

16. A
17. B
18. C
19. A
20. C

21. Prior to the 1986 Independence Bowl victory, when was the last year Ole Miss won a bowl game, and who was the opponent?
A. 1971 Peach Bowl vs. Georgia Tech
B. 1970 Sugar Bowl vs. Arkansas
C. 1968 Liberty Bowl vs. Virginia Tech

22. This sophomore placekicker connected on a 48-yard, fourth-quarter field goal in the 1986 Independence Bowl, points that proved to be the difference in an Ole Miss three-point victory.
A. Neil Teevan
B. Bryan Owen
C. Hoppy Langley

23. Who scored the Rebels' two touchdowns in the 1986 Independence Bowl?
A. Willie Goodloe and Joe Mickles
B. John Fourcade and Joe Gunn
C. Mark Young and Buford McGee

24. The 1987 Rebels, Billy Brewer's fifth team since his return as head coach, were thought by some preseason prognosticators to be his best to that point. However, an extremely disappointing three-win season followed. Name the three teams the Rebels defeated.
A. Memphis State, Arkansas State, Tulane
B. Arkansas State, Southwestern Louisiana, Vanderbilt
C. Southwestern Louisiana, Vanderbilt, Mississippi State

25. Ole Miss finished off a 5-6 rebuilding season in 1988 with a walloping of Mississippi State in Jackson. What was the final score?
A. 33-6
B. 34-7
C. 35-3

---

21. A
22. B
23. A
24. B
25. A

26. The 1989 season was Coach Billy Brewer's seventh back at his alma mater. It was also his finest to that point. What was the Rebels' record in the regular season of '89?
A. 9-2
B. 7-4
C. 8-3

27. Ole Miss won at Memphis State 20-13 to open the 1989 season, and in game two the Rebels defeated a Southeastern Conference opponent 24-19 on the road. Name that foe.
A. Georgia
B. Alabama
C. Florida

28. Against Florida in 1989, this Ole Miss defender intercepted two Gator passes — one for a touchdown and another to set up a touchdown. Name him.
A. Chauncey Godwin
B. Gerald Vaughn
C. Cassius Vaughn

29. The Rebels' starting quarterback in 1989 was a senior from Corinth, Mississippi. Who was he?
A. Jim Weatherly
B. John Darnell
C. Russ Shows

30. Ole Miss started the 1989 season 3-0, but an unlikely opponent almost won game three. The Rebels prevailed over this team 34-31 in Oxford.
A. Southwestern Louisiana
B. Southeastern Louisiana
C. Arkansas State

---

26. B
27. C
28. A
29. B
30. C

31. After losing back-to-back games to Arkansas and Alabama, the 1989 Ole Miss Rebels rebounded by winning a thriller in Oxford against a tough SEC foe. Name the team and the final score.
A. Auburn: 21-17
B. Georgia: 17-13
C. Tennessee: 20-14

32. This Rebel tight end caught the game-winning pass against Tulane in the Louisiana Superdome with four seconds remaining in the game for a 32-28 Ole Miss victory in 1989.
A. Kris Mangum
B. Rich Gebbia
C. Wesley Walls

33. Against Tulane in New Orleans in 1989, one of the smallest Rebels on the squad had arguably the biggest performance, with a 43-yard touchdown reception, a kickoff return of 38 yards, a 47-yard punt return, and two receptions on the game-winning drive – all in the fourth quarter. Name him.
A. Pat Coleman
B. J.R. Ambrose
C. Eddie Small

34. Homecoming 1989 was a 24-16 victory for Ole Miss, but the day is painfully remembered as the game Rebel defender Chucky Mullins was severely injured. Name the opponent that afternoon.
A. Vanderbilt
B. Tulane
C. Middle Tennessee State

---

31. B
32. B
33. A
34. A

35. Ole Miss needed a win over MSU in 1989 in the Battle for the Golden Egg to finish the regular season on a positive note. The Rebels had lost to LSU and Tennessee the previous two games. What was the final score of the '89 Egg Bowl in Jackson?
A. 21-9
B. 21-11
C. 20-12

36. Ole Miss defeated a service academy team to wrap up the 1989 season. Who was the opponent, what was the final score, what was the bowl, and what was the Rebels' final record?
A. Army, 27-13, Independence, 7-5
B. Navy, 31-14, Peach, 9-3
C. Air Force, 42-29, Liberty, 8-4

37. The season opener in 1990 was significant for more than simply a 23-21 Ole Miss victory over Memphis State. What was that significance?
A. It was the first football game played on the Ole Miss campus in August
B. It was played on Labor Day afternoon
C. It was the first night football game at Ole Miss after lights were installed that summer

38. In the third game of the 1990 season, Ole Miss beat Arkansas 21-17 in Little Rock. What was the famous play called that sealed the win when the Rebels' Chris Mitchell finished off Razorback ball-carrier Ron Dickerson just short of the end zone after he was hit by fellow defenders Chauncey Godwin and Shawn Cobb?
A. "The Hit"
B. "The Stop"
C. "The End"

---

35. B
36. C
37. C
38. A

39. In late October 1990, the Rebels escaped Nashville with a squeaker over Vanderbilt to continue their excellent season. What was the final score?
A. Ole Miss 10, Vandy 9
B. Ole Miss 31, Vandy 30
C. Ole Miss 14, Vandy 13

40. The Rebels' last two wins of the regular season in 1990 were over rivals LSU (19-10) and MSU (21-9). With a record of 9-2, Ole Miss was invited to what Florida bowl game to play what Big Ten team?
A. Citrus vs. Ohio State
B. Gator vs. Michigan
C. Orange vs. Northwestern

41. An Ole Miss junior placekicker made five field goals in the season opener of 1991, a 22-3 UM win at Tulane. Name this kicker.
A. Bryan Owen
B. Steve Lindsey
C. Brian Lee

42. Ole Miss began the 1991 season 5-1. What was the Rebels' final record?
A. 5-6
B. 7-4
C. 9-2

43. The Battle for the Golden Egg moved back to the campus stadiums beginning in 1991 after several seasons in Jackson. What year had the game moved to the capital city from the campus sites?
A. 1972
B. 1973
C. 1974

---

39. C
40. B
41. C
42. A
43. B

44. What former Clemson head coach served on Billy Brewer's staff as offensive coordinator and quarterbacks coach for four seasons?
A. Red Parker
B. Danny Ford
C. Frank Howard

45. The 1992 Ole Miss football team was one of the most successful of the Billy Brewer era. Who was the starting quarterback?
A. John Darnell
B. Lawrence Adams
C. Russ Shows

46. The 1992 Ole Miss Rebels finished with nine wins, which included a bowl victory. What bowl game did they play in, whom did they beat, and what was the score?
A. Sun Bowl, Arizona, 21-0
B. Liberty Bowl, Air Force, 13-0
C. Cotton Bowl, Oklahoma State, 14-0

47. Two of the team's three losses in 1992 were to traditional powers Alabama and Georgia. The other setback was a surprisingly lopsided loss to another SEC program. Who was the team and what was the score?
A. Vanderbilt: 31-9
B. Arkansas: 27-7
C. Kentucky: 28-10

48. This Rebel running back gained nearly 1,000 yards (994) in 1992. Who was he?
A. Cory Philpot
B. Marvin Courtney
C. Dou Innocent

---

44. A
45. C
46. B
47. A
48. A

49. What Rebel offensive lineman was named first-team All-American in 1992 but had been a walk-on when he first played in 1989?
A. Todd Wade
B. Matt Luke
C. Everett Lindsay

50. What year was Billy Brewer's last season as head coach at Ole Miss?
A. 1994
B. 1993
C. 1995

---

49. C
50. B

TUBERVILLE AND CUTCLIFFE ERA

1. In 1994, Ole Miss had an interim head coach who served as the Rebels' defensive coordinator in 1993. Who was he?
A. Jim Carmody
B. Joe Lee Dunn
C. Robert Henry

2. The most significant victory for Ole Miss during the 1994 season was on Homecoming Day in Oxford. The Rebels won 34-21. Whom did they beat?
A. Auburn
B. Alabama
C. LSU

3. The Rebels' starting quarterback during the 1994 season was a talented signal-caller from southern California who had transferred to Ole Miss from Fullerton (California Community) College. Name him.
A. Josh Nelson
B. Paul Head
C. Jeremiah Masoli

4. Ole Miss went looking for a new head coach before the 1995 season. Texas A&M's defensive coordinator was the choice. Who was the Rebels' new head coach?
A. Tommy Bowden
B. Tommy Tuberville
C. Tommy Luke

---

1. B
2. C
3. A
4. B

5. The Rebels had a 1-1 record through two games in 1995 when an SEC power arrived in Oxford. Ole Miss got the win by an 18-10 final, and the new era had begun in a big way. Whom did the Rebels defeat?
A. Auburn
B. Alabama
C. Georgia

6. In that third game of the 1995 season, the Rebels' placekicker proved to be the player of the game after connecting on four field goals. Who was this kicker?
A. Steve Lindsey
B. Tim Montz
C. Les Binkley

7. In the Egg Bowl of 1995, won by Ole Miss 13-10 in Starkville, the Rebels had a running back who gained 242 yards and ran all over the Bulldogs. Name this star of the game.
A. Dou Innocent
B. John Avery
C. Joe Gunn

8. Ole Miss played many football games in the capital city of Jackson in its 125-year history. However, the last time the Rebels played there was the second game of the 1996 season. Who was the opponent and what was the final score of the Rebel win?
A. Idaho State, 38-14
B. Virginia Military Institute (VMI), 31-7
C. Arkansas, 19-0

---

5. C
6. B
7. A
8. B

9. The Rebels' biggest win during the 5-6 season of 1996 came on November 23 at Georgia. What was the final score of this road game?
A. 21-17
B. 20-13
C. 31-27

10. Broc Kreitz and Walker Jones chased down this Georgia player to prevent a touchdown and preserve the victory for the Rebels in 1996. The play began at the Georgia 1-yard line as the player caught a pass from quarterback Mike Bobo, then raced to the Rebel 16-yard line where he was caught. The Bulldog, who didn't score on the play, went on to star in the NFL. Who was it?
A. Matthew Stafford
B. Garrison Hearst
C. Hines Ward

11. After the 1996 season, the Rebels' tight end was named first-team All-American. Name this native Mississippian who went on to a successful NFL career.
A. Wesley Walls
B. Kris Mangum
C. Rufus French

12. The Rebels entered the 1997 season with much optimism and promise. Even in their first game, the season was perhaps saved with an overtime victory. Ole Miss won 24-23 in Oxford. Who was the opponent?
A. Memphis
B. Florida
C. Central Florida

---

9. C
10. C
11. B
12. C

13. The opposing quarterback in the 1997 season opener went on to a successful career in the NFL. But on this night he fell just short of the winning two-point conversion in overtime, literally stumbling and landing inches from the Rebel goal-line. Who was this talented signal-caller?
A. Paxton Lynch
B. Danny Wuerffel
C. Daunte Culpepper

14. Ole Miss hosted a university from Texas in Oxford for game two of the 1997 season. Who was the foe?
A. Texas Tech
B. Houston
C. Southern Methodist (SMU)

15. The signature win of the 1997 campaign was a 36-21 mid-season victory over this highly-ranked opponent on the road.
A. LSU
B. Florida
C. Georgia

16. In a rare Thursday night mid-season televised game from Oxford, Ole Miss won 19-9 before a national audience, showcasing the talented 1997 Rebels. Whom did they beat?
A. Vanderbilt
B. Tennessee
C. Arkansas

---

13. C
14. C
15. A
16. C

17. Although already bowl eligible in 1997, Ole Miss needed a victory in the Egg Bowl in Starkville to make certain of more football during the holiday season. They got it with a 15-14 win over the Bulldogs. Who threw the pass and who caught the football on a two-point conversion with 25 seconds to go in the game?
A. Lawrence Adams to Eddie Small
B. Stewart Patridge to Cory Peterson
C. Paul Head to Roell Preston

18. Before there was a two-point conversion with 25 seconds left for victory in the 1997 Egg Bowl, there had to be a touchdown play. Who caught a 10-yard touchdown pass to pull the Rebels to within one point?
A. Andre Rone
B. Rufus French
C. Willie Green

19. Ole Miss played in a bowl game for the first time in five seasons in 1997 when the Rebels traveled to this city for postseason play. Name this locale.
A. Jacksonville – Gator Bowl stadium
B. Shreveport – Independence Bowl stadium
C. Detroit – Pontiac Silverdome

20. Who was the Rebels' opponent in its 1997 bowl game?
A. Nebraska
B. Oklahoma
C. Marshall

21. What was Ole Miss's final record after the 1997 season?
A. 8-4
B. 7-5
C. 9-3

---

17. B
18. A
19. C
20. C
21. A

22. Current Ole Miss head coach Matt Luke was one of the co-captains of the 1998 Rebel squad. Who was the other?
A. Deuce McAllister
B. Cory Peterson
C. Gary Thigpen

23. The Rebels traveled to Dallas to play SMU in late September 1998. Trailing 41-19 entering the fourth quarter, this Rebel returned a punt for a touchdown to start a comeback for Ole Miss.
A. Cory Peterson
B. Vincent Brownlee
C. Marshay Green

24. The Rebels beat SMU in overtime in Dallas in 1998. What was the final score?
A. 47-41
B. 48-41
C. 48-44

25. Where was the miracle comeback in Dallas played when Ole Miss beat SMU in overtime in 1998?
A. On the SMU campus
B. Texas Stadium
C. Cotton Bowl stadium

26. The Texas-Oklahoma football game is always played the weekend of another big event in Dallas. That same event was going on outside Cotton Bowl stadium in 1998 when Ole Miss and SMU played there. What was the event?
A. South by Southwest Festival
B. The Texas State Fair
C. Dallas Festival of the Arts

---

22. C
23. A
24. B
25. C
26. B

27. The last Ole Miss victory of the 1998 regular season was a 37-31 thriller in overtime. Whom did the Rebels beat that Halloween afternoon in Oxford?
A. Tennessee
B. LSU
C. Arkansas

28. After the Mississippi State game of 1998, Tommy Tuberville and his staff left Ole Miss for Auburn. Who was named the Rebels' head football coach a few days later?
A. Tennessee Assistant Coach David Cutcliffe
B. Clemson Head Coach Tommy West
C. Middle Tennessee State Head Coach Boots Donnelly

29. Quarterback Romaro Miller was injured the week before the 1998 Egg Bowl in a game at Georgia and was unavailable to play in the regular-season finale. What was the name of the freshman backup quarterback who started and played against Mississippi State?
A. David Morris
B. Jevan Snead
C. Jake Hill

30. The Rebels were 6-2 through eight games of the 1998 season but finished 6-5. That still qualified them for a bowl game. Where did they play?
A. Music City Bowl
B. Liberty Bowl
C. Independence Bowl

31. Ole Miss won its 1998 bowl game 35-18. Who was the opponent?
A. Texas A&M
B. Texas-El Paso
C. Texas Tech

---

27. B
28. A
29. A
30. C
31. C

32. Months before the 1999 football season began, Ole Miss signed its quarterback of the future. Who was he?
A. Seth Smith
B. Eli Manning
C. Doug Zeigler

33. After Ole Miss beat Memphis 3-0 in the regular-season debut for David Cutcliffe, the first-year head coach was asked by a reporter if he was "disappointed with the score since he is an offensive-minded coach." Which of these quotes was his response?
A. "I'm not ever disappointed with a victory."
B. "Three-point wins are fine with me; just win."
C. "What I am is a winning-minded coach."

34. Ole Miss played at Auburn in the fourth game of the 1999 season – the Rebels' former coach, Tommy Tuberville, then at Auburn, vs. their new coach, David Cutcliffe. How did the game turn out?
A. Ole Miss won 28-21 in regulation
B. Ole Miss won 24-17 in overtime
C. Auburn won 24-23 in overtime

35. What college football coaching legend did Ole Miss beat when his South Carolina team fell to the Rebels 36-10 in Columbia, S.C., on October 2, 1999?
A. Steve Spurrier
B. Lou Holtz
C. Paul Dietzel

---

32. B
33. C
34. B
35. B

36. Ole Miss's last two wins of the regular season in 1999 were against two rivals by lopsided margins: 42-23 and 38-16. Name the two schools the Rebels defeated.
A. LSU and Arkansas
B. LSU and Mississippi State
C. Arkansas and Mississippi State

37. Ole Miss defeated Oklahoma 27-25 in the 1999 Independence Bowl on a game-winning field goal as the contest concluded. What dependable Rebel placekicker put the victory points on the scoreboard?
A. Brian Lee
B. Bryan Owen
C. Les Binkley

38. The 2000 Rebels were supposed to have the manpower to win a championship, but some difficult losses prevented that from happening. Still, Ole Miss had some important wins on its way to a 7-5 final record — like on Homecoming Day in Oxford by a 43-40 margin in overtime. Who was the foe?
A. Tulane
B. UNLV
C. Louisiana-Monroe

39. The Rebels qualified for the 2000 Music City Bowl by winning the Battle for the Golden Egg vs. MSU in Oxford. What was the final score?
A. 45-30
B. 42-31
C. 38-21

---

36. A
37. C
38. B
39. A

40. Romaro Miller, Deuce McAllister, and Derrick Burgess were three of the four-team captains in 2000. Name the other captain for the Rebels that season.
A. Eli Manning
B. Shane Elam
C. Ken Lucas

41. With the Rebels trailing 49-16 in the second half of the 2000 Music City Bowl, Coach David Cutcliffe inserted redshirt freshman quarterback Eli Manning, who proceeded to bring his team back. Three drives later, all resulting in Manning touchdown passes, the Rebels lost only 49-38. Who won the game that day?
A. Michigan State
B. West Virginia
C. Minnesota

42. The 2001 season was tragically interrupted by the 9/11 attacks on the World Trade Center in New York. Ole Miss stood 1-1 after the weekend of September 8. The Rebels didn't play another game for three weeks for two reasons — nationally all games the weekend of September 15 were postponed, and Ole Miss had a previously scheduled open date on September 22. Who was Ole Miss's opponent on September 29, 2001, what was the location, and what was the final score of the Rebel victory?
A. Arkansas State, Jonesboro, Ark., 35-17
B. Kentucky, Lexington, Ky., 42-31
C. Alabama, Oxford, Miss., 27-24

43. The Ole Miss game that was postponed on September 15, 2001, after the 9/11 attacks, was played on December 1, 2001, in Oxford. Who was the opponent and what was the final score of the Rebel victory?
A. Tulane, 29-22
B. Southeastern Louisiana, 38-14
C. Vanderbilt, 38-27

---

40. B
41. B
42. B
43. C

44. During the 2001 season, Ole Miss and Arkansas played the longest game in NCAA history by periods to that point. How many overtimes were played that night, and what was the final score of the Razorback victory?
A. Six overtimes, 60-56
B. Seven overtimes, 58-56
C. Eight overtimes, 64-62

45. On October 5, 2002, Ole Miss claimed a headline-worthy 17-14 victory against Florida in Oxford. The goalposts came down and made their way to the Grove and on to the Square after the Rebels' big win, with eager students doing the heavy lifting. Eli Manning quarterbacked Ole Miss that day. Who was the Gators' quarterback?
A. Rex Grossman
B. Ingle Martin
C. Chris Leak

46. Ole Miss had to defeat Mississippi State in the 2002 Egg Bowl to become postseason bowl eligible. They did so by what final score?
A. 24-12
B. 17-10
C. 20-9

47. In the 2002 Independence Bowl, the Rebels beat this team 27-23. Who was it?
A. Baylor
B. Air Force
C. Nebraska

---

44. B
45. A
46. A
47. C

48. Lanier Goethie, Doug Zeigler, and Eddie Strong were three of the four team captains in 2002. The other one was the center on the offensive line who snapped the football to quarterback Eli Manning. Name him.
A. David Vinson
B. Ben Claxton
C. Thomas Kimbrough

49. In 2002 Ole Miss lost a regular-season road game to Texas Tech, and its high-powered offense, which was led by this all-star quarterback turned NFL head coach.
A. Graham Harrell
B. B.J. Symons
C. Kliff Kingsbury

50. For the 2002 season, Vaught-Hemingway Stadium was expanded with the completion of the south end zone grandstands, club seats, and suites. What was the official capacity for the stadium from 2002 through 2015?
A. 60,580
B. 60,150
C. 60,789

51. The 2003 season was anticipated across Rebel Nation like few others since the early 1970s. The season opener was unusual in that it was played on the SEC road, and that proved to be a late August challenge. Ole Miss won, but it wasn't easy. Who was the road opponent, and what was the final score?
A. Kentucky, 20-17
B. Vanderbilt, 24-21
C. Auburn, 27-24

---

48. B
49. C
50. A
51. B

52. In the season opener of 2003, the game's final points were off the foot of this Rebels placekicker. How long was Jonathan Nichols' game-winner with less than five minutes to go in the contest?
A. 54 yards
B. 57 yards
C. 49 yards

53. The Rebels were 2-2 and a successful 2003 season hung in the balance as Ole Miss played another SEC road game. The Rebels moved to 2-0 in the SEC with a victory at this difficult place. Where was it, who was the opponent, and what was the final score?
A. Athens, Georgia, 16-13
B. Knoxville, Tennessee, 17-14
C. Gainesville, Florida, 20-17

54. After a 55-0 win against Arkansas State in 2003 on Homecoming, Ole Miss hosted Alabama the next week. Outrushing the Crimson Tide 216 yards to 116, the Rebels dominated from start to finish. What was the Rebels' SEC record after the 43-28 win over Alabama?
A. 4-0
B. 5-0
C. 3-0

55. Ole Miss was 6-0 in conference games when LSU arrived at Vaught-Hemingway Stadium in 2003. The Tigers fell behind in the first quarter, but when the day was done, LSU prevailed 17-14. What movie star led Rebel Nation in "Hotty Toddy" prior to the historic contest?
A. Brad Pitt
B. Tom Hanks
C. Russell Crowe

---

52. A
53. C
54. C
55. C

56. Ole Miss easily bounced back from its loss to LSU by winning big on the SEC road at Mississippi State the following week. What was the final score?
A. 31-0
B. 35-0
C. 38-0

57. The loss to LSU in 2003 meant a co-championship of the SEC West for the Rebels but no trip to Atlanta for the title game. Ole Miss still managed an invitation to a prestigious postseason game. What bowl did the Rebels play in following the '03 regular season?
A. Sugar
B. Cotton
C. Outback

58. Whom did Ole Miss face in the bowl game after the 2003 season, and what was the final score of the Rebels' victory?
A. Oklahoma State, 31-28
B. Oklahoma, 30-24
C. Texas, 34-30

59. Eli Manning finished third in the Heisman Trophy balloting after the 2003 season but did pick up another prestigious national award as the College Player of the Year. Name that award.
A. The Griffin Award
B. The Rockne Award
C. The Maxwell Award

60. One of Eli Manning's backup quarterbacks went on to a highly successful career in Major League Baseball. Name this Mississippian.
A. Jake Hill
B. Jay Hepfer
C. Seth Smith

---

56. A
57. B
58. A
59. C
60. C

61. Following the 2003 season, Ole Miss placekicker Jonathan Nichols won what award indicative of the nation's best player at that position?
A. The Lou Groza Award
B. The Cloyce Hinton Award
C. The Tom Dempsey Award

62. Rebel Nation was stunned after the 2004 team lost its season opener at home. Who beat Ole Miss and what was the final score?
A. Tulane, 21-14
B. Memphis, 20-13
C. Louisiana-Lafayette, 19-17

63. The Rebels never recovered from a season-opening loss in 2004 and moved on to a surprisingly mediocre season with only four wins. Whom did Ole Miss beat?
A. Vanderbilt, Arkansas State, Wyoming, Mississippi State
B. Vanderbilt, Arkansas State, South Carolina, Mississippi State
C. Vanderbilt, Arkansas State, Tennessee, Mississippi State

64. Ole Miss played three quarterbacks throughout the 2004 season. Who was this signal-calling trio?
A. Micheal Spurlock, Robert Lane, Ethan Flatt
B. Bo Wallace, Chad Kelly, Randy Karliner
C. Dan Patch, Seth Smith, David McKinney

65. After the 4-7 season of 2004, Ole Miss relieved its head coach of his duties and named an assistant from another powerhouse program to replace him. Name the two men.
A. David Cutcliffe and Will Muschamp
B. Tommy Tuberville and David Cutcliffe
C. David Cutcliffe and Ed Orgeron

---

61. A
62. B
63. B
64. A
65. C

ORGERON AND NUTT ERA

1. Ole Miss won its 2005 season opener at Memphis, but there were only a few wins after that. Name the teams the Rebels also defeated in 2005.
A. The Citadel and Kentucky
B. VMI and Vandy
C. Army and Mississippi State

2. The Alabama game of 2005 in Oxford was there for the taking, but the Rebels couldn't finish. Ole Miss lost by what score?
A. 14-7
B. 21-20
C. 13-10

3. In 2006 the Rebels won their season opener again. Whom did they beat that day by a final score of 28-25?
A. Ohio University
B. Presbyterian College
C. Memphis

4. Patrick Willis was one of two team captains in 2006. Who was the other?
A. Andrew Wicker
B. Kyle Wicker
C. Trey Wicker

5. Ole Miss played an Atlantic Coast Conference (ACC) team at home in 2006 and played the same team again on the road two seasons later in 2008. Name this team.
A. Duke Blue Devils
B. North Carolina State Wolfpack
C. Wake Forest Demon Deacons

---

1. A
2. C
3. C
4. A
5. C

6. Just like the "almost" win against the Crimson Tide during the 2005 season, Ole Miss almost beat Alabama in Tuscaloosa in 2006. What was the final score of this overtime Rebel loss?
A. 20-17
B. 26-23
C. 14-13

7. Ole Miss finished a four-win 2006 season with a victory in the Egg Bowl. Where was that game, won by the Rebels 20-17, played?
A. Jackson
B. Starkville
C. Oxford

8. In 2007 Ed Orgeron's program made it three straight against Memphis in season openers, beating the Tigers again, this time 23-21. They would win only two more games that season and go winless in the SEC. Name the two teams besides Memphis the Rebels defeated in 2007.
A. Louisiana-Monroe and Louisiana-Lafayette
B. Louisiana Tech and Northwestern (Louisiana) State
C. Southeastern Louisiana and Nicholls State

9. Ed Orgeron made a call to go for it on fourth down at his team's own 49-yard line at Mississippi State with the Rebels leading 14-0 in the fourth quarter. Ole Miss failed to make the first down, and when the game was over, the Bulldogs had a 17-14 victory. What happened to Orgeron the following day?
A. His contract was extended, and he coached a fourth season in 2008
B. His contract was not extended, but he coached a fourth season in 2008
C. He was relieved of his duties as the Rebels' head coach

---

6. B
7. C
8. B
9. C

10. Ole Miss stayed within the SEC family for its next head coach. Whom did the Rebels hire?
A. Former Vandy and LSU head coach Gerry Dinardo
B. Former Arkansas head coach Houston Nutt
C. Former Auburn head coach Terry Bowden

11. The going was bumpy early for the 2008 Rebels. The brightest moment of the first half of the season came on September 27 in an SEC road game. Whom did the Rebels beat 31-30, and who was that team's quarterback?
A. Florida and Tim Tebow
B. Alabama and Greg McElroy
C. Auburn and Cam Newton

12. After starting the 2008 season 3-4, the Rebels rolled through five consecutive wins to end the regular season 8-4. Name the teams Ole Miss defeated in that stretch.
A. Wake Forest, Vanderbilt, Auburn, LSU, Mississippi State
B. South Carolina, Louisiana-Lafayette, Auburn, LSU, Mississippi State
C. Arkansas, Auburn, Louisiana-Monroe, LSU, Mississippi State

13. Ole Miss beat up on its two biggest rivals – LSU and MSU – to wrap up the 2008 regular season. Name the final scores of those two November games.
A. 31-13 vs. LSU and 45-0 vs. MSU
B. 30-10 vs. LSU and 46-3 vs. MSU
C. 28-7 vs. LSU and 48-6 vs. MSU

14. Ole Miss defeated an 11-win Texas Tech team 47-34 in the last Cotton Bowl game played in Cotton Bowl Stadium in Dallas on January 2, 2009. Who coached the Red Raiders that day?
A. Spike Dykes
B. Kliff Kingsbury
C. Mike Leach

---

10. B
11. A
12. C
13. A
14. C

15. Ole Miss started 2-0 in 2009 with blowout wins against Memphis and Southeastern Louisiana. Then came a 16-10 upset loss on the SEC road. Who beat the Top 5 ranked Ole Miss Rebels that night?
A. Arkansas
B. South Carolina
C. Georgia

16. Ole Miss throttled Tennessee 42-17 on November 14, 2009, in Oxford. How many yards and touchdowns did Dexter McCluster have that day for the Rebels?
A. 324 all-purpose yards and four touchdowns
B. 310 all-purpose yards and five touchdowns
C. 319 all-purpose yards and three touchdowns

17. In a thriller on November 21, 2009, Ole Miss won a home game 25-23 against an SEC opponent with some help from the opposing coaching staff's late-game clock management or the lack thereof. Who was this visiting foe?
A. Arkansas
B. Mississippi State
C. LSU

18. For the second straight postseason, Ole Miss played in the Cotton Bowl – this time on January 2, 2010. But unlike the year before, the game was played in the new Cowboys Stadium in Arlington, the first Cotton Bowl game played outside of Dallas. Whom did Ole Miss defeat 21-7 that day?
A. Oklahoma
B. Kansas State
C. Oklahoma State

---

15. B
16. A
17. C
18. C

19. The Houston Nutt era hit the skids early in 2010. On opening day a team from Alabama beat Ole Miss 49-48 in two overtimes in Oxford. Rebel Nation still cringes when this team is mentioned.
A. North Alabama
B. Jacksonville State
C. South Alabama

20. Ole Miss bounced back in game two of 2010 with a victory over its oldest opponent, the only team it still plays that it also played in the first season of football in 1893. Name this team.
A. Memphis
B. Tulane
C. Southern Mississippi

21. In 2010 Ole Miss made a long-distance trip to the West Coast to play a team. The Rebels won 55-38. Whom did they beat?
A. Fresno State
B. California-Berkeley
C. UCLA

22. In 2010 a transfer quarterback from Oregon played in every game for Ole Miss. Who was this talented signal-caller?
A. Marcus Mariota
B. Jeremiah Masoli
C. Joey Harrington

23. The 2011 season began in Oxford. Picking up where they left off in 2010, the Rebels lost a close contest 14-13. Who was the opponent?
A. UAB
B. VMI
C. BYU

---

19. B
20. B
21. A
22. B
23. C

24. The Rebels won just two of 12 games in 2011, the worst season in decades. When was the last time prior to 2011 that Ole Miss had won as few as two football games in a season?
A. 1946
B. 1915
C. 1895

25. This offensive lineman was one of the Rebel team captains in 2011 and has had a lengthy career in the NFL. In 2019 he is listed as a tight end with the Chicago Bears. Name this Mississippian.
A. Todd Wade
B. Matt Luke
C. Bradley Sowell

26. This running back was one of the Rebel team captains in 2011 and has had a successful career in the NFL, mostly with the New England Patriots. Who is he?
A. Brandon Bolden
B. Joe Gunn
C. Ben Jarvus Green-Ellis

---

24. A
25. C
26. A

FREEZE AND LUKE ERA

1. After a third consecutive loss to Mississippi State, Houston Nutt was relieved of his coaching duties at Ole Miss. Hugh Freeze replaced Nutt. What former Ole Miss head coach's staff had Freeze been on?
A. David Cutcliffe
B. Ed Orgeron
C. Tommy Tuberville

2. Freeze won his first game at Ole Miss 49-27 to open the 2012 season in Oxford. Whom did the Rebels beat?
A. Central Arkansas
B. Arkansas Tech
C. Arkansas State

3. UTEP was the second victim of the Freeze era, falling to the Rebels 28-10. A former head coach at Alabama was the Miners' head coach that day. Who is he?
A. Mike Shula
B. Mike DuBose
C. Mike Price

4. On October 13, 2012, the Freeze-era Rebels won their first SEC game, a 41-20 victory against this team (The win snapped a lengthy 16-game SEC losing streak for Ole Miss).
A. Arkansas
B. Auburn
C. Texas A&M

---

1. B
2. A
3. C
4. B

5. Ole Miss beat Mississippi State 41-24 in 2012 to become bowl eligible. What bowl did the Rebels participate in following the regular season?
A. Liberty Bowl in Memphis
B. Independence Bowl in Shreveport
C. Compass Bowl in Birmingham

6. Who was Ole Miss' bowl opponent in Birmingham on January 5, 2013, and what was the final score of the Rebels' victory?
A. Houston, 45-19
B. Pittsburgh, 38-17
C. Tulsa, 41-21

7. The 2013 season opened in Nashville as the Rebels played at Vanderbilt. Sealing the 39-35 Ole Miss victory was a 75-yard run for a touchdown late in the game by this Rebel running back.
A. Jeff Scott
B. Jordan Wilkins
C. Brandon Bolden

8. Ole Miss traveled to Austin, Texas, on September 14, 2013, to face the Texas Longhorns, who had won the year before in Oxford. Not this time. Ole Miss claimed a win by what final score?
A. 48-24
B. 49-27
C. 44-23

9. Ole Miss finished the 2013 season in the same city it had started the campaign – Nashville, Tennessee. The finale was a victory for the Rebels in the Music City Bowl against this ACC team.
A. Georgia Tech
B. Pittsburgh
C. Virginia

---

5. C
6. B
7. A
8. C
9. A

10. Ole Miss opened the 2014 season in one of the preseason showcase games, this time in the Chick-Fil-A Kickoff Classic against Boise State in Atlanta. The Rebels won, but what was the score?
A. 35-14
B. 35-13
C. 35-10

11. Ole Miss and Vanderbilt played the following week in 2014, but this time it wasn't at Dudley Field on the Vandy campus. The game was in the NFL home of the Tennessee Titans. It was a mismatch as Ole Miss rolled.
A. 41-3
B. 42-3
C. 45-3

12. Bo Wallace was in his third season as the Rebel starting quarterback and had firmly cemented himself as one of the SEC's best signal-callers of the era. Where is Bo Wallace from, and what high school did he attend?
A. Lewisburg, Tennessee; Marshall County High
B. Lawrenceburg, Tennessee; Lawrence County High
C. Pulaski, Tennessee; Giles County High

13. On October 4, 2014, this ESPN show made its Grove debut prior to the Ole Miss-Alabama football game.
A. College Gameday
B. Touchdown TV
C. College Football Pregame

14. Who won the game and what was the score of the Ole Miss-Alabama game in 2014?
A. Ole Miss, 21-13
B. Alabama, 16-14
C. Ole Miss, 23-17

---

10. B
11. A
12. C
13. A
14. C

15. On October 11, 2014, Ole Miss won a football game at this locale for the first time ever.
A. Waco, Texas
B. Lubbock, Texas
C. College Station, Texas

16. This SEC team served as a Homecoming feast for Ole Miss in 2014. The game wasn't close as the Rebels won big, 34-3. Who lost to Ole Miss that day?
A. Kentucky
B. Tennessee
C. South Carolina

17. To solidify a spot in a "New Year's Six Bowl" at the end of the 2014 season, Ole Miss had to win the Egg Bowl in Oxford. They did so by what final score?
A. 34-20
B. 30-16
C. 31-17

18. With its 9-3 record, Ole Miss headed to a bowl in the same city where it had started the 2014 season — Atlanta. The Rebels won against Boise State in August. But in the Peach Bowl, they lost to what team?
A. SMU
B. TCU
C. BYU

---

15. C
16. B
17. C
18. B

19. Although it was against inferior competition, Ole Miss showed in its first two games of 2015 just what potential it had that season. Scoring more than 70 points in each game, the Rebels beat what two teams in Oxford to begin the '15 season?
A. South Alabama and Southeast Missouri State
B. Tennessee-Martin and Fresno State
C. New Mexico State and Chattanooga

20. The 2015 Rebels rolled into Tuscaloosa, Alabama, with a 2-0 record. For the second year in a row, Ole Miss was victorious against the Crimson Tide. Quarterback Chad Kelly connected with this receiver for a 24-yard touchdown completion to give Ole Miss a 43-24 lead before Alabama made a late run.
A. Laquon Treadwell
B. Cody Core
C. Quincy Adeboyejo

21. After back-to-back losses, the 2015 Rebels faced a critical game at home on October 24. What SEC team did Ole Miss defeat 23-3 that day to right its slipping ship?
A. Auburn
B. Texas A&M
C. LSU

22. The most painful game of the 2015 season was arguably a loss to this SEC team in Oxford. The contest went into overtime, and only a miracle fourth-and-25 play which the opposition converted kept the visiting team's hope alive. The loss likely kept Ole Miss out of the SEC Championship game in Atlanta. Who beat Ole Miss 53-52 that day?
A. Missouri
B. Kentucky
C. Arkansas

---

19. B
20. A
21. B
22. C

23. On November 28, 2015, Ole Miss and Mississippi State played in Starkville for the right to go to the Sugar Bowl in New Orleans. MSU was looking for its first appearance in the Classic, while the Rebels were playing to go for the ninth time. Chad Kelly outdueled Dak Prescott, and Ole Miss got the trip to the Big Easy with a 38-27 win. What was the Ole Miss lead at the end of the first quarter?
A. 21-0
B. 17-0
C. 24-0

24. What was the halftime lead for the Rebels in the 2015 Egg Bowl won by Ole Miss 38-27?
A. 24-3
B. 24-6
C. 28-3

25. After MSU closed the gap to 31-13 in the 2015 Egg Bowl through three quarters, this Rebel ran for 38 yards and a touchdown early in the fourth period for a 38-13 UM advantage.
A. Chad Kelly
B. Jordan Wilkins
C. Jaylen Walton

26. The Sugar Bowl was all Rebels. Whom did Ole Miss defeat 48-20 in New Orleans on January 1, 2016?
A. Oklahoma
B. Texas
C. Oklahoma State

---

23. A
24. C
25. B
26. C

27. The Rebels were making their ninth appearance in the Sugar Bowl on January 1, 2016. How long had it been since the eighth Sugar Bowl appearance for Ole Miss?
A. 43 years
B. 46 years
C. 49 years

28. Chad Kelly won the Miller-Digby Trophy on January 1, 2016. What's this award signify?
A. The SEC Football Sportsmanship Award
B. The top quarterback in the SEC
C. It's given to the MVP of the Sugar Bowl

29. Ole Miss has played in the Sugar Bowl nine times. How many times have the Rebels won it?
A. Six
B. Five
C. Four

30. The ninth Sugar Bowl game for Ole Miss was played in the Louisiana Superdome. The other eight appearances the Rebels made in the New Orleans holiday classic were in another venue. Name it.
A. Tad Gormley Stadium
B. City Park Stadium
C. Tulane Stadium

31. The 2016 football season at Ole Miss was a disappointment. The final record was 5-7, this coming off a 10-win Sugar Bowl campaign in 2015. One highlight was in Oxford when the Rebels beat Coach Kirby Smart's first Georgia team. What was the final score?
A. 42-21
B. 45-14
C. 38-13

---

27. B
28. C
29. A
30. C
31. B

32. In 2016 Ole Miss won for the second time in a row at this Texas venue. The final score was 29-28 Rebels, and it was their last win of the season. Who was the opposition?
A. Texas A&M
B. Texas
C. TCU

33. The largest crowd in Vaught-Hemingway Stadium/Hollingsworth Field history was in 2016 when 66,176 was announced for what game?
A. Auburn
B. Alabama
C. Georgia

34. Hugh Freeze was relieved of his duties as head coach in the summer of 2017. Who took over the program?
A. Derrick Nix
B. Tom Luke
C. Matt Luke

35. The inaugural class of the Sugar Bowl Hall of Fame was announced in 2017. Ole Miss had two in that first group of 16. Name them both.
A. Glenn Cannon and Chad Kelly
B. Raymond Brown and Archie Manning
C. Jake Gibbs and Bobby Ray Franklin

36. Ole Miss made a rare football appearance at a Pac-12 campus during 2017. Where did the Rebels play a football game on September 16 of that season?
A. Tucson, Arizona
B. Eugene, Oregon
C. Berkeley, California

---

32. A
33. B
34. C
35. B
36. C

37. A struggling Ole Miss team in 2017 put it all together against Vanderbilt in Oxford. What was the final score of the Rebels' victory?
A. 57-35
B. 49-14
C. 45-21

38. Quarterback Jordan Ta'amu connected with wide receiver D.K. Metcalf on a 7-yard touchdown pass with five seconds to go in the game, and Ole Miss won 37-34 on the road in the SEC on November 4, 2017. Who was the opponent?
A. Tennessee
B. Kentucky
C. Alabama

39. Ole Miss beat Mississippi State again in Starkville in 2017. What was the final score?
A. 30-27
B. 32-29
C. 31-28

40. In 2017 Ole Miss dedicated an extended portion of the Walk of Champions from the Grove to Vaught-Hemingway Stadium. What Rebel great is the area named for, and what group does it recognize?
A. The A.L. Bondurant Student-Athlete Pavilion
B. The Jake Gibbs Letterwinners Walk
C. The Harry Mehre Champions Patio

41. Who won the Conerly Trophy, presented to the top college football player in Mississippi, in 2017?
A. A.J. Brown
B. D.K. Metcalf
C. Jordan Ta'amu

---

37. A
38. B
39. C
40. B
41. A

42. Ole Miss head coach Matt Luke played his high school football where in Mississippi?
A. Biloxi
B. Long Beach
C. Gulfport

43. Matt Luke's brother, Tom, played for Ole Miss under Coach Billy Brewer. What position did Tom Luke play?
A. Placekicker
B. Quarterback
C. Offensive Lineman

44. Ole Miss opened the 2018 season with a 47-27 win over Texas Tech in what Texas city?
A. Lubbock
B. Arlington
C. Houston

45. The Rebels beat Arkansas 37-33 in this rivalry game that in 2018 was played in which Arkansas city?
A. Little Rock
B. Fayetteville
C. Jonesboro

46. For the 2019 season, Rich Rodriguez was named offensive coordinator for the Rebels. He had been the head coach at three major conference schools. Name them.
A. Wake Forest, Rutgers, Arizona State
B. West Virginia, Michigan, Arizona
C. Wisconsin, Kansas State, UCLA

---

42. C
43. B
44. C
45. A
46. B

47. For the 2019 season, Mike McIntyre was named defensive coordinator for the Rebels. He had been the head coach at a Pac-12 university. Name that school.
A. Utah
B. Washington State
C. Colorado

48. Ole Miss hosts a Pac-12 university in Oxford during the 2019 season. Name that school.
A. Washington
B. Oregon State
C. California-Berkeley

49. Ole Miss's starting quarterback in 2019 is Matt Corral, a freshman from what western state?
A. California
B. Arizona
C. Nevada

---

47. C
48. C
49. A

RECORDS & MISCELLANEOUS

1. Who holds the record for most touchdown passes in a single game?
A. Eli Manning
B. Chad Kelly
C. Charlie Conerly

2. Which Ole Miss player holds the record for most field goals kicked in a game (six)?
A. Gary Wunderlich
B. Robert Khayat
C. Jonathan Nichols

3. During a single game, an Ole Miss player racked up a school record 540 total offensive yards against Alabama. Name the player.
A. Eli Manning
B. Archie Manning
C. Chad Kelly

4. Dexter McCluster broke the Ole Miss record for most rushing yards in a single game against Tennessee in 2009. How many rushing yards did McCluster gain?
A. 282 yards
B. 210 yards
C. 180 yards

5. Which Ole Miss player holds the record for most completions in a single game (42)?
A. Jordan Ta'amu
B. Eli Manning
C. Shea Patterson

---

1. A
2. C
3. B
4. A
5. B

6. Eli Manning holds the record for consecutive completions in a single game. What is that number?
A. 15 completions
B. 18 completions
C. 22 completions

7. Which Ole Miss player holds the record for most passing yards in a game (489)?
A. Shea Patterson
B. Chad Kelly
C. Eli Manning

8. Which Ole Miss player punted for over 500 yards against Florida in 2002, shattering the record for most punt yards in a game?
A. Cody Ridgeway
B. Bill Smith
C. Jim Miller

9. Mike Wallace holds the record of most kickoff return yards in a single game (v. Vanderbilt in 2008). How many return yards did Wallace gain?
A. 168
B. 112
C. 202

10. Which Ole Miss player holds the record for all-purpose yards (rushing and receiving) in a single game (324)?
A. Dexter McCluster
B. Deuce McAllister
C. Charlie Flowers

---

6. B
7. A
8. A
9. C
10. A

11. Who holds the record for most points scored in a season? And what position does he play?
A. Jonathan Nichols, kicker
B. A.J. Brown, wide receiver
C. Deuce McAllister, running back

12. The record for most rushing touchdowns in one season is held by four different players: Brandon Bolden, John Dottley, Archie Manning, and Deuce McAllister. How many touchdowns does each player have?
A. 12
B. 14
C. 18

13. Eli Manning is one of two players tied for the most passing touchdowns in a season (31). Who is the other player?
A. Jordan Ta'amu
B. Jimmy Lear
C. Chad Kelly

14. The Ole Miss record for most passing touchdowns caught in a season is 11. Two players hold the record. Which player listed below does not hold the record?
A. Laquon Treadwell
B. A.J. Brown
C. Barney Poole

15. Who holds the record for most extra points in a season with 63?
A. Jonathan Nicoles
B. Gary Wunderlich
C. Luke Logan

---

11. A
12. B
13. C
14. C
15. B

16. Which Ole Miss player shattered the offensive record book when he generated 4,542 yards in a single season?
A. Chad Kelly
B. Eli Manning
C. Jordan Ta'amu

17. Which Ole Miss player holds the record for most rushing yards in a season (1,312)?
A. Deuce McAllister
B. John "Kayo" Dottley
C. Dexter McCluster

18. Kayo Dottley holds many of the Ole Miss rushing records, including the best average yards rushing per game in a single season (131). But Dottley doesn't hold the best average yards per rush during a season. Which Ole Miss star averaged 7.4 yards per carry during the 1957 season?
A. Raymond Brown
B. Kent Lovelace
C. Charlie Flowers

19. Eli Manning holds the record for most passing attempts in a season (481), but who holds the record for most pass completions during a season?
A. Chad Kelly
B. Bo Wallace
C. John Fourcade

20. Stewart Patridge holds the Ole Miss record for most consecutive passes without an interception. What is Patridge's record?
A. 124
B. 200
C. 81

---

16. A
17. B
18. C
19. A
20. B

21. Which Ole Miss quarterback holds the record for most passing yards in a season (4,042)?
A. Eli Manning
B. Chad Kelly
C. Archie Manning

22. Which Ole Miss quarterback holds the record for most yards passing per game in a season (326)?
A. Jordan Ta'amu
B. Chad Kelly
C. Eli Manning

23. Two Ole Miss quarterbacks are tied for most interceptions thrown in a single season (20). Who are they?
A. Eli Manning and Archie Manning
B. Eagle Day and Chad Kelly
C. Jevan Snead and John Fourcade

24. Which Ole Miss quarterback holds the record for most 300-yard passing games during a single season (9)?
A. Chad Kelly
B. Jordan Ta'amu
C. Eli Manning

25. Which Ole Miss player holds four single-season records for receiving, including most receptions (85), receptions per game (7.1), total yards (1,320), and yards per game (110)?
A. A.J. Brown
B. Laquon Tredwell
C. D.K. Metcalf

---

21. B
22. A
23. C
24. B
25. A

26. What Ole Miss player holds the record for most tackles during a season (168)?
A. Patrick Willis
B. Ben Williams
C. Jeff Herrod

27. What was Coach Vaught's overall record as a head coach at Ole Miss?
A. 202-51-10
B. 190-61-12
C. 162-87-14

28. Two Ole Miss players, Senquez Golson and Bobby Wilson, hold the record for most interceptions in a single season. What is the single-season record?
A. 10
B. 8
C. 6

29. The record for most yards returned on interceptions in a single season (162) is held by which Ole Miss player?
A. Glenn Cannon
B. Senquez Golson
C. Junie Hovious

30. Which Ole Miss player holds the record for most career games as a starter (49)?
A. Marcus Tillman
B. Tre' Stallings
C. Micheal Oher

---

26. C
27. B
28. A
29. B
30. A

31. Which Ole Miss player holds the record for most career points scored (350)?
A. Archie Manning
B. Chad Kelly
C. Gary Wunderlich

32. Which Ole Miss player holds the record for most touchdowns scored in a career (41)?
A. Dexter McCluster
B. Deuce McAllister
C. Kayo Dottley

33. Which Ole Miss quarterback holds the record for most touchdown passes thrown in a career (81)?
A. Eli Manning
B. Charlie Conerly
C. Chad Kelly

34. Which Ole Miss kicker holds the record for most consecutive extra points made in a career (117)?
A. Gary Wunderlich
B. Jonathan Nichols
C. Josuha Shene

35. Which Ole Miss wide receiver holds the record for most career touchdown passes caught (24)?
A. A.J. Brown
B. Laquon Tredwell
C. Chris Collins

---

31. C
32. B
33. A
34. B
35. C

36. Who holds the record for most field goals in a career (63)?
A. Joshua Shene
B. Jonathan Nichols
C. Gary Wunderlich

37. Which Ole Miss player holds the record for most career offensive yards (10,478)?
A. Bo Wallace
B. Eli Manning
C. Chad Kelly

38. The record for total career rushing yards (3,060) is held by which Ole Miss running back?
A. Joe Gunn
B. Dexter McCluster
C. Deuce McAllister

39. Who holds the record for most games with 100+ yards rushing?
A. Kayo Dottley
B. Joe Gunn
C. Deuce McAllister

40. One Ole Miss player holds three of the top records for career passing: most passes (1,363), most completions (829), and most passing yards (10,119). Who is that quarterback?
A. Eli Manning
B. Chad Kelly
C. Bo Wallace

---

36. B
37. A
38. C
39. C
40. A

41. Which Ole Miss quarterback holds the record for most consecutive games with a touchdown pass (22).
A. Bo Wallace
B. Chad Kelly
C. Eli Manning

42. Which Ole Miss receiver holds the career record for most passes caught (202)?
A. Laquon Treadwell
B. Evan Engram
C. Chris Collins

43. Which Ole Miss receiver holds the career record for most receiving yards (2,984)?
A. Laquon Treadwell
B. Shay Hodge
C. A.J. Brown

44. Which Ole Miss player holds the Ole Miss and SEC record for career pass interceptions (20)?
A. Bobby Wilson
B. Glenn Cannon
C. Senquez Golson

45. Which Ole Miss punter holds the SEC record for most punts over 50 yards in a career (88)?
A. Jim Miller
B. Bill Smith
C. Gary Wunderlich

---

41. B
42. A
43. C
44. A
45. B

46. Which Ole Miss punter holds the career records for most punts (266) *and* most punt yards (11,549)?
A. Bill Smith
B. Merle Hapes
C. Jim Miller

47. Which Ole Miss player holds the record for most punt return yards in a career (1,142)?
A. Jason Armstead
B. Junie Hovious
C. Doug Cunningham

48. Which Ole Miss player holds the record for most kickoff return yards in a career (2,036)?
A. Mike Wallace
B. Jaylen Walton
C. Jesse Grandy

49. Which Ole Miss player holds the school record for most tackles in a career (528)?
A. Jeff Herrod
B. James Stuart
C. Patrick Willis

50. Which Ole Miss player holds the SEC record for most sacks in a career (37)?
A. Marquis Haynes
B. Greg Hardy
C. Ben Williams

---

46. C
47. B
48. B
49. A
50. C

51. The 1992 Battle for the Golden Egg in Oxford, won by Ole Miss 17-10, became known by what name because of the tremendous defensive effort by the Rebels in the fourth quarter?
A. The Stop
B. The Stand
C. The Real Deal

52. What name has been given to the Ole Miss-LSU game played each football season?
A. The River Bowl
B. The Rivalry
C. The Magnolia Bowl

53. How many SEC championships has Ole Miss won in football?
A. Six
B. Five
C. Seven

54. What is the name of the indoor football facility and training center for Ole Miss football?
A. The IPF
B. The Olivia and Archie Manning Athletics Performance Center
C. The Ole Miss Football Complex

55. What is the name of the prestigious award given to an outstanding Rebel defensive player in the spring each year?
A. The No. 38 Award
B. The Chucky Mullins Courage Award
C. The Rebel Defender

---

51. B
52. C
53. A
54. B
55. B

Made in the USA
San Bernardino, CA
11 December 2019

61201687R00063